The Nerve

GLYN MAXWELL

The Nerve

HOUGHTON MIFFLIN COMPANY

Boston   New York   2002

For Geraldine
and for Alfreda

Copyright © 2002 by Glyn Maxwell

For information about permission to reproduce selections from this book, write to Permissions, Houghton Mifflin Company, 215 Park Avenue South, New York, New York, 10003.

Visit our Web site: www.houghtonmifflinbooks.com.

Library of Congress Cataloging-in-Publication Data is available.
ISBN 0-618-15546-5

Book design by Melissa Lotfy
Typeface: Electra

Grateful acknowledgment is made to the following publications, in which some of these poems originally appeared: *Agenda, Agni Review, Bostonia, Last Words: New Poetry for the New Century* (Picador, UK), *Matrix, Metre, The New Yorker, Ploughshares, Poetry Review* (London), *Qualm, Rattapallax, Short Fuse,* and the *Times Literary Supplement.*

"A Child's Love Song" was written for the marriage service of Isabelle Bedu and Anthony Sycamore.

Printed in the United States of America

QUM 10 9 8 7 6 5 4 3 2 1

CONTENTS

THE SEA COMES IN LIKE NOTHING
BUT THE SEA

The sea comes in like nothing but the sea,
but still a mind, knowing how seldom words

augment, reorders them before the breaker
and plays them as it comes. All that should sound

is water reaching into the rough space
the mind has cleared. The clearing of that mind

is nothing to the sea. The means whereby
the goats were chosen nothing to the god,

who asked only a breathing life of us,
to prove we were still there when it was doubted.

THE NERVE

Somewhere at the side of the rough shape
your life makes in your town,
    you cross a line,
    perhaps

in a dusty shop you pause in, or a bar
you never tried, and a smell
    will do as well;
    then you're

suddenly very far from what you know.
You found it as a child,
    when the next field
    to you

was the world's end, a breeze of being gone.
Now it begins to give,
    a single nerve,
    low down:

it sags, as if it felt the gravity
at long last. You are chilled
    to have been told
    that way—

but you ought to recognise it, it's the one
that may well fail one day,
    fail utterly,
    go wrong,

be Judas, while the others, without thought
of you, or of your pain,
        show no sign,
        are mute,

assume they're safe with you. Treasure the nerve
suggesting otherwise;
        treasure its dis-
        belief:

it's straining to see the outline of somewhere
inhospitable,
        with other rules,
        unfair,

and arbitrary, something to endure,
which nonetheless you spot,
        contemplate,
        start for;

where you will face the choices that the nerve
has suffered: to be plucked
        and, for that act
        of love,

to have brought the soldiers running; to lie low,
and, for that act of fear,
        have perished years
        ago.

HAUNTED HAYRIDE

At the near edge of the field, a dollar a shot,
the hay cart waited with its horse and man,
handing the children on and their mothers on,
unhanding them to a place on a hay-cart seat,

swivelling for the next. The field was a farm
beginning by Route 9, a mile at most
from town and our life here. It seemed to us
it was all farm to the start of the next farm.

It was selling its things to everyone whose plans
had ground to a stop on the road that afternoon.
Round here if you stop long enough, then *boom*—
tall women come in cardigans and jeans

and everything's a stall. Car passengers,
grey and fit and buckled in there, lifers,
all turned back to their sentences, but whatever
opens unexpectedly to strangers

possessed us, so we slowed, and stopped. The hay cart
was both the farthest and the first of things
we saw, beyond the gift shop selling pumpkins
for luck, and ghosts and Indians for mascots.

So instead we ambled up towards the sign,
making an M with Alfie's arms, Maxwells,
past pumpkin heaps and jars on the hay bales,
towards the horse and cart and the hay-cart man.

He handed the children on and the mothers on,
and cleared a space for three, till it felt to us
like the gap was suddenly waiting for us, and this
intervened. And the look on the hay-cart man

intervened. So did the scope of the field,
stretching away from Saturday like a hand,
out into Massachusetts, towards England,
into the past, and from it. The air filled

with cold and we chose pumpkins at a stall.
Two, and two toys for Alfie. There was a card
explaining what their dollar for the cart
would get them: it would get them a ghost tale,

some spookiness in daytime. It had rolled
by then, that wagon. I could see its pale
brown halted speck from the highway, as if hell
were littleness, and they were being told.

THE MAN WHO HELD HIS FUNERAL

Rugged and silken, like a country singer
both those things, fastidious and scary,
yet fitted by the terms of his employment
in a sober suit and driving gloves, he seemed
defeated in a civil war still going.

He said he'd lived his life. What was he, sixty?
with children and grandchildren, his car business
solid, sold. He laid his leather hands
on the steering wheel and said he'd lived his life.
And so one day had held his funeral.

Although he looked in his blue single-breasted
right for one, we caught each other's eyes
and tried to find this funny or him funny.
It depended. All his pals had been invited,
had come from far and wide and there he lay,

face-up in a hired coffin, taking breaks
for Pepsi while he listened to their speeches.
Which, by the grin I saw in the driver's mirror,
must have delighted him on his bed of satin,
staring with eyes closed. Oh they made cracks,

he told us, they hit home, they didn't spare me!
We didn't really know how to receive this,
in the back, on the winning side, except politely,
then without words to stretch back and imagine
his friends were probably mourning him, you'd have to,

because he hadn't died, because he'd held
his funeral, to hear the case against him,
but had heard nothing and was satisfied,
and reassured that all the things he loved
and strolled among had had their hour of judgment.

GATEKEEPERS ON DANA

The first act
of the first light in the east
is to make gatekeepers of those great twin pines
on Dana Street:

to find them,
the needs and fissures in them,
make heralds of them, the first of all to affirm
by their aspect

the emergency,
or chillingly to imply
the amplitude of what's to come. When it's gone,
what it is,

and you wonder
what cranks the shadows round
together like the beasts at a long feeding,
who, finishing,

move off,
don't try to ask that pair,
because if you do they will ask themselves, *What gate
has he in mind?*

then brush and murmur,
Why would it need keeping?
Shiver and hazard: *Are you expecting something?*
Tell all.

ONE OF THE SPLENDOURS

The bloom between blue-pink and cherry-pink
on our north wall was new, began, was out—
one of the splendours made to make us think
it's time to learn some names. We'd done without
      since coming here in winter, in the grey.

The bird with the three semitones, the bird
that seems to be half air, the butterfly
that seems to be half everything but word—
we sat and thought, It's time. It is our house.
      We won't, though, I know us. We like to see

stuff strain at us from nothing, through the space
alarm in kind or colour or degree,
be there, not have been there and appear now—
then yellow at the wall in the few days
      following, and fail not knowing how.

Or be the bird long gone though its song weighs
on in us, be dead, be oceanbound
for all we know. We rest on all we know,
our little bench, and watch the trees around
      in turn unsettle, like an hour ago.

TODAY

Today will trail a warm hand at his side,
sweep the stone wall, brush the bushes,
clobber along the bars and redden and ring,
returning to his pocket.

Today keeps on. When he glances back, if need be,
it's only to see grow through the bars
and wave like waterlife the unnumbered pleading
hands of one-time colleagues.

A WINTER EVENING

Night fell on afternoon, which had been slow
as herded animals, with their deep feelings.
Beliefs had come of those, and in the chitchat
and diplomatic interim of evening

they are recalled. Respectful are the smiles
that greet them, but the tiniest of teaspoons
tips the sugar in, and for miles around
the dark is stationed.

BLINDFOLD

Far down below, what is in all but truth
the sea lights on Chicago in the dawn.
Waves whiten. Utter distance holds the breath,
as if by any ocean. Boats down there
    look tiny, lone
    and fierce as the first stars.

Blindfold a boy, a woman, set them there:
divest their eyes and watch them see the sea,
the fools; observe them smell salt on the air,
the fools. They might be musing on an iceberg,
    race memory
    afresh on that horizon,

but we who only visit it know more,
and knowledge won't take nothing for a view.
We castellate the line, we feel land there,
cold fishing ports and cousins we could phone,
    drive to, fly to;
    we talk it to a loop,

and the dreaded sky to airways. Yet we find
at points all morning, at the earthly hours,
the disabused, those of a former mind:
salt at the nostril, mortified by heights
    of fang-black towers —
    they're beggared by the speed

at which after a cent or passing word
their loneliness smacks back in shape like rubber.
Contrariwise went things. The centigrade
will winnow these with skill, as will our hands
        which sort the copper
        coins for the most worthless,

until one comes who's not in on the secret,
in whose eye there is nothing but *whose eye*,
one whom the light unwittingly makes sacred,
who knows no bounds and nothing else, who drops
        from the white sky
        rope ladders that start shaking.

REFUGEES IN MASSACHUSETTS

Everyone had to leave in a bloody hurry.
No one had to come here. Those who did—
the ones who should be sorry were not sorry.
The ones who shouldn't be

run restaurants or laundromats or serve you
shyly in the mall. Exquisite hands
show you your change. Or chattily they drive you
when you're too tired to say,

when all the diddy icons on the dashboard
tremble. It's your town and not your town
when you leave tips for them. What's barely whispered
where they meet is true:

they might encounter him from the old world,
who came at night, who giggled at their papers . . .
Might see him smoking by the baseball field,
padding towards the diner,

lip-reading in the library. That man
escaped here, he too sobbed or stared ahead,
made landfall; he eats pretzels in the line.
They are aware he's there

both when he is and isn't there. No crimes
will stick in the new life. There is no court
in session for the narratives and claims
their voices split to make,

no angles to examine. There are times
they jump and times they clasp. There is a wood
they come to in a downpour, or have dreams
they come to in a downpour.

THE YEAR IN PICTURES

For the Year-in-Pictures feature,
that annual old favourite,
the man behind the night desk

was dealing with five thousand
possibles at high speed,
a speed at which his blond head

was shaking and his fingers
propelling off so many
the air was never empty

of the white-backed and numbered
snapshots, as they fluttered
earthward in succession.

FARM ANIMALS ARE CHILDHOOD

Farm animals are childhood. As we bike past
Massachusetts cows, we can't imagine
anything but English — England's version —
smouldering in a cow brain like compost.

Bikes are childhood. We forked out for these
to ride along this dotted path. The roads
aren't childhood here, so anyone who rides
must overhaul whole biking dynasties.

On a deserted stretch one afternoon
the sun shone and we braked where two small boys
and a big girl were stooping in the trees
beside a fence. The cows stood farther on,

vaguely following things with Dorset eyes.
Watching children isn't childhood. Stones
we watched hit the cow flanks, and the cow minds
pieced it together, reckoning otherwise,

as the missed stones fell still and were believed.
Believing's childhood. Caring isn't quite,
and we did more than that, though we did squat,
cared about it, fretted over calves,

phoned the police, the calf police, some hour
later. They're not childhood on the phone.
Childhood is a well a mile from home,
in which things go on falling till they're here.

A HUNTING MAN

Nothing but snow about. A hunting man
set out from his own truck and his sleeping son,

who followed him, found no one, and was found
five days later frozen to the ground.

His father had been nothing but a fool.
He went about his chores, he went to school

for nothing, and he waited in his truck.
The days were featureless and the nights black

he drove into. He hunted in that place,
he camped there in the trees, he heard the ice

shifting in the branches. "Not the best,"
his sister told a lady from the press,

"the thing he did," and chatted on the path.
But he'd assured her that his Christian faith

prevented him from carrying out his will.
A judge considered thirty days in jail

appropriate for manslaughter. The man
dissented, and some yards from where his son

was found he shot himself. Nothing but snow
about, nothing but trees, nowhere to go.

Peace is as poor a word for what he has
as *silence* is for what it signifies.

Justice softens to sweet nothings here.
Love holds its own, admit it, as before.

CHARTREUSE

A kid in glasses, sceptical
like kids in glasses, I'm the one
in Double Art, still staring at
grey paper, while our teacher

is informing us a grey sky
is anything at all but grey:
Just look at it, she's singing, *pinks,
greens, blues, chartreuses* . . .

I look. I look again at both
the sky she means and the scrawled word
chartruese (my hand's up) on the board
she's turning from, triumphant.

The kids are lining up small pots
like factories. The sky I see
is grey, though when I see her face
I falter, forget it,

then ask why can't I leave it blank,
since that's grey. She hurries round,
distracted with concern, and briskly
handing me the colours.

A PROMISE

I made my child a promise, so a weight
was passed to her. I saw how carefully

its power was handled, that it lit the thoughts
around it, and I felt it warm her talk

and urge the hours along. Since I, like you,
no longer know a word like that, the light

she gained was lost to me. It didn't mean
I'd let her down — I didn't — but I seemed

to be aligned with those who might in time,
as if I'd somehow set coordinates.

TWO BREATHS

Alfie on Christmas Eve. Her breath is caught,
    let out in shots,
unsettled and unique with thinking things
    we said will happen.

My breath, expecting nothing, is so calm
    it measures time,
or passes for it, so if time could hear
    it would hear silence.

A CHILD'S LOVE SONG

Thumb and finger make a ring
       to see the future through.

I can see the world through it,
       only the world and you,

only the world and you alone.
       If I should break this ring,

where will I find you in the world
       though I find everything?

ISLAND PAINTING, ST. LUCIA

Once under the one hoisted tent of noon
we set to watercolours in the shade;
I went for green and dabbed it on too soon,
    I made limeade
    of every water glass.

The ever-painted island let a towel
of shadow round it till it all was dry;
our teacher looked and set a lasting vowel
    down as I
    uncapped ultramarine.

Recurring errors I could term a style,
I joked to you and made one as I did,
where the still-damp wash was tipped with wet detail
    and all was blurred
    to blazes. I sat back:

already you were starting on the tree
I judged beyond me; you had three pale ochres
working on it. I had a midnight sea
    with violet breakers
    (which were not the case),

and, cheating, I had had the horizon ruled,
though still it fizzled; yours was the true line
that draws a beam on the retreating world,
    is the one sign
    we learn from its long passing.

Your brushes idled in their Evian;
mine mutinied in ink. Our teacher watched
his ocean darken. "Not too heavy on —
        too late." He reached
        his hand out to his island,

gravely observed the cartoon foliage
I'd heaped on it, then riffled through my pad
to the relieving cool of a blank page.
        At least I had
        one picture true to light.

When he was gone my palette boiled with browns
unknown to man; I mixed at it until
I found one colour true among the stains;
        upon the hill's
        dark back I added that.

The hour came to meet the green you made
too soon this morning, you were ready now,
leaf-confident. My move into deep red
        had ended how
        all movies end, all wrong.

The sky I'd dawdled over was a blue
it wouldn't recognise as one. The clouds
I'd given it were gaps; they were the few
        shapes in God's
        heaven that can't be clouds

and can't be helped. How much of this can be?
The water in the glass can look like water,
the brushes be made pure, and steadily
      held towards the
      island, the sharp pencil

can judge the distance. We can do this better,
render the remaining thing before
there are no colours, and our patient teacher
      comes to the door
      to offer fish or chicken.

The lamps went on and things were cleared away.
We swapped our works and liked each other's most
for what had spoiled them. So was the best day
      over. The west
      had finished too, its piece

a squinting four-eyed creature, two right arms
extended to the evening sea, each
bearing a pencil, framed by the olive palms
      of one who'll teach
      the simple things for ages.

THE PAVING STONES
For Geraldine

Between a spring and a river with a name,
there'll be a place it curves and the water flinches,
        is barely ruffled in its stream
of light, is a lady smoothing out her sleeve,
but she's been clipped, and you in a 1960s

stroller let your head bow down, your chin
lodge on the rail your mittens hold, and your eyes
        watch the parading space and line
and space and line recur in the paving stones
so close below. It mills and mesmerises,

and you still have it, earlier than a sound,
sweet as either hand: through the long days
        it scurries under, still a ground
passing. If you stain it for a moment,
it means to say, a line is what arises.

THE ONLY WORK

In memory of Agha Shahid Ali

When a poet leaves to see to all that matters,
nothing has changed. In treasured places still
     he clears his head and writes.

None of his joie-de-vivre or books or friends
or ecstasies go with him to the piece
     he waits for and begins,

nor is he here in this. The only work
that bonds us separates us for all time.
     We feel it in a handshake,

a hug that isn't ours to end. When a verse
has done its work, it tells us there'll be one day
     nothing but the verse,

and it tells us this the way a mother might
inform her son so gently of a matter
     he goes his way delighted.

THE POEM RECALLS THE POET

This is for him, the writer, him I term
the creature of two feet, for he'd present
his face two feet away. He made a warm
glow to see by, willing and well meant,
but not, I'd have to say, for the long haul.
Things he began were things I'd have to end,
I sensed immediately. When I recall
the touch of what he did with his near hand,

the mood comes over me, but the mood goes,
and that reminds me too. November days
the thought of him resolves into a voice
that states it matters now—so does the wind,
but neither moves a muscle of my face
before it dies as if it read my mind.

THE WEATHER GUY

Hurricane This is scaring us,
Hurricane That's not far behind,
and we're not turning our backs one second.
We look at the screen all day. We find

Hurricane This still flapping away
at the shirt of Tom the Weather Guy.
Canada throws an arm around him.
Hurricane That just bats an eye.

Hurricane This is whipping off
the Carolinas' tablecloth;
Hurricane That, amused by this,
is beating ocean into froth.

Hurricane This is playing wolf
to New York City's clever pig;
Noah's nailing down his roof
so when it comes it's nothing big.

Hurricane This is burning out
off Providence; Hurricane That
is disappointing Tom, who'd dreamt
of half Virginia pounded flat.

And Hurricane This was called Renee.
And Hurricane That was Stan.
And Canada pats Tom's shoulder now
as he hands us back to Jenni-Ann,

who asks about his weekend plans,
which are much the same as ours,
so maybe we'll see him nosing out
of a local brawl of cars,

and maybe he'll give us the wave he gets
when the heat kicks in and how,
and it hits the heights he said it would
this far upstate by now.

More likely he'll just speed away.
And I'd be shy of the love
of those who have to live by what
I have to warn them of.

AN EARTHLY CAUSE

Because against the brown of the wide heath
out there that afternoon the shape was small
and pallid, bare and still,
it could have been a body: for a while
it was. When it resolved
into a pair of them, the pair of us

fell to explaining them: that they were young,
no second thought, that they were girl and boy,
they did appear to be,
in love of course, to sit so far away,
have walked so far in such
persistent heat, to have to have so far

to trek back to this path was a notch for love.
We had had days of sun and weeks of sun.
If this affair began
when that began, that would have seemed a sign,
a deal of two good hands,
a garden tended for them. As the dawns

continued foggy, burning off by nine,
belief would harden to a sense of fate,
in retrospect at that,
noon their witness, noon their intimate,
passing them ahead
to noon again, till what they'd happened on

would seem to have been waiting. Such a faith
can make it to the winter, but the days
continued hot. Today
was one of them, incensing heat, a sigh
that is all *s*. Our minds
were on to them, we couldn't let them be,

not now. Their attitude, in the tall tale
we spun as we walked on, should sour and turn
against the light, the sun
itself fall into question, a dry plain
spread before them, distance
measure what they had. If the heat stayed

relentlessly they'd find an earthly cause
at hand to blame, associate their lives
with that, hear old beliefs
and blush to. They were picking up their stuff
by now: we hurried on
along the path in patterns of late sunlight.

THE ALUMNI

The best of them have blown in to the former
patch, to the Bronze-and-Green,
and thread along the sunbeams in the Tavern
to group at the wiped table in their corner.

And they notice as they sit around the window,
how the bottles and old prints
are as before, as is the ancient joke
they share to laughter's steep diminuendo,

which levels to a murmur in the haze.
The drinks come and they peer
intently in them, stir the ice. The check
arrives, and loudly each insists it's his.

They tour Schaff Field behind a bright young lady,
half of them always dawdling.
They disagree on dates but never meaning;
half satirise, half not, a sense of story,

and celebrate as if it were the present,
however brief the looks
that meet them passing Ingram Chapel, looks
of planetary beauty, equidistant.

The cobbled paths converge in the old pattern,
meet at the stone passage.
No choice but single file; they call out names.
All is echo then, till all is sunshine.

The bright young lady stops the group and points
to the Class of '50 gym,
where they oversee the first engraving ever
of certain words in marble, that moment,

the cutter at their middle names, their '50
in central pride of place,
as the driller drills a ring of stars around them,
and the bright young lady reads until they're ready.

THE LEONIDS

The corners of our eyes,
cold and alert to missing them, report
a flash, and in the breeze
    we turn our heads
to where the stars are quiet.

It goes against the grain,
to understand what's next is going to shoot
from anywhere. The brain,
    seeing a thing
so like itself, falls flat.

Leonids. A word,
as if they had some source or destiny,
as if this utmost speed
    they hurtle at
were theirs—towards, away—

and not our burning loop
that lights the dust they are. As if this date
were something that they keep,
    appointment reached
neither too soon nor late,

but punctual to the end.
Leonids. *Our word, our speed, our date,*
bawls the affronted mind,
    shaking the fixed
stars this way and that.

STOPIT AND NOMORE

Being the entire word-hoard of "Genie"
(see various accounts) when she was found.
"Genie" indeed. World on a rushing wind,
    three wishes!
thumped back in a bottle that was empty.

She floated through the wards with her own wake
of the dumbstruck, her hands bunched like paws
below a perfect face. Her Cerberus
    of a parent
primed his gun and scribbled his last bark.

She was thirteen. Given everything, she thrived,
was told the names for this and that, it seems
too late for them to hold. She lived in homes
    belonging
to scientists and carers, then she lived

in foster homes. It went to court. In time
it fell to her exonerated mother
to take her back. And back she went forever.
    I found her
cited in a book I read, *Genome*,

proving what she proves, or at least supports,
though some say it's too muddied by the life
to pass for science. I say words arrive
    too late
for love, or love is gone too soon for words.

LIKES AND DISLIKES

A late night at the bureau, midnight oil
of various flavours sampled, the cool light
of laptops on their faces, the new unit
    pooled ideas,
until an all-American young girl

took shape. They each had turns at being her,
the others firing questions, till by dawn
they had enough. They met their chief at noon,
    and gazed out
at the city with him. Then they took a car

downtown to celebrate. They raised a glass
to her in every place. She went to work
that night. She listed all her likes and dislikes,
    her do's and don'ts.
A chance remark about a favourite dress

elicited a hit. The unit cheered,
set down their coffees, and approached the screen.
Another question came from the same man,
    and he was toast
for sure. He made a date and what appeared

was a short adult agent in pink sneakers.
He beat it on a technicality,
because his victim was a nobody,
    literally,
if fondly recollected by her makers.

CROW AND CALF AND DOG

Elizabeth Knapp of Groton, farmer's daughter,
possessed (though you may use the cooling tongs
of quote marks on "possessed"), stuck out her tongue
     one sabbath,
and backed the men assembled to all corners.

The sounds of crow and calf and dog came out.
She was a farmyard, and the worse she got,
the more they watched her in the candlelight
     for any sign
she knew them, but her eyes were rimmed and wet.

"Oh, you are a rogue," she told the preacher.
"You are a great black rogue. You tell the people
a company of lies." The men, though fearful,
     feared God,
and fought their corners with ferocious Scripture,

rooks in chess. They heard their Christian names
in a croaked accent. "This is my pretty girl!"
She wiped her face: "I've been here for a while,"
     to which
the preacher bellowed: "God has you in chains!"

and in turn the girl replied: "For all my chains
I can knock thee on the head if I so please."
Which was all that she could think of, or her voice
     could hold,
or the language had. She bit into her hands.

THE GAME ALONE

The Purple School and its sworn enemy
contend again. I sidle in among those
        seeing it: alumni of the Purple,
and opposite numbers—literally, each class
in Magic Marker: womenfolk of '70
        proffer pies in frilled tents, in an oval

round the patterned field. I stroll a lap
in coat and scarf along the generations,
        '80, '64, grey men in sportswear,
already smiling at the leading question,
and thirty autumns pass as they look up
        to hear announcements crackling from somewhere.

One mascot's like a man, one's like a bull.
The man's huge plaster head is done to look
        colonial, bewigged; he's on the side
of everyone I'm sitting with, for luck,
while they deride him over there, they howl
        and make bull horns, bent fingers to the head.

The Purple flag flies here. Both sides of course
are cheer-led by those girls and by this brute
        who stomps along the stand in a tracksuit,
bellowing at the old folks to support.
Below, the game goes on and a side scores.
        I think of asking how and decide not;

it suddenly feels like asking television,
though television knows. In fact I change,
        stroll round, become a White-on-Scarlet guy,
why not. Our chant is going up—"Revenge!"—
and a row of girls, all blond and loyal and frozen,
        try joining in just as it dies away.

I notice, when the game is in its times
of rest (again), that this whole bank of people
        is gazing out across the churning river,
at a world where what is white is coloured purple,
but otherwise all's well. A fresh face beams
        to see its twin, souls gladden with a shiver.

From far away, from that wide field away,
the bucket-headed mascot from the past
        turns all the rest to background. It's a game,
you want to say when seeing him, when faced,
and your skull small. The stands and hills and sky
        go darker than expected in the time,

for there's a light that it can seem the game
alone is generating. A great cheer
        on mine—the bull side—and it almost ends,
with the old-timers wobbling up to roar,
vocabulary boiled down to a name,
        and it does end, when thirty-seven seconds

vanish from the screen—a voice confides,
They're running down the clock—far over there,
     the crowd leaps up, and over here it sits.
The field lets go its lines; it doesn't care
who scampers on to form the ring of weeds
     around a violet mushroom-crop of helmets,

or the off-white and muddy red melee
disintegrating to some weary boys
     bareheaded between parents. Now it's cold
and finished. Down among the beaten guys
three girls are searching. All their jerseys say
     ATHLETICS in the dusk. They find and hold

their treasures, 45, 8, 84,
and try to speak that body language, bowed
     dismay, though in a secret swirl of joy
to be the one despondent at his side.
The winners melt away and can have more.
     The losers hold the field. Too suddenly

for some here comes the Purple flag, the guy
is taunting us—not us, I mean my side—
     by streaming it below our wooden stand,
lording it with something not quite pride,
more personal, all his. As he runs by,
     this White-on-Scarlet, talking with a friend,

shoots out a hand that gets it, jerks the cloth
half off its stick, and stops him in his track.
      I'm very near. The victor is amazed
that happened and is grinning but in shock,
his eyes wondering *What now?* They are both
      lost for an act. The third one's realised,

and, setting free the flag, averts a scene.
So the bearer wanders on, unsure, long fields
      between him and his home. No one close by
knows quite what's to be done with what he feels;
they file away in time, treading the green
      homewards, passing strangers on the way,

contemporaries from the long-rivalled school,
or their own schoolmates who were in the future.
      All things have been exchanged, and I can't see
by now who'd cheered for what. It seems much darker
than anyone could play in. A tall girl
      is carrying the bull mask by the eye,

and as I look back nothing in the stands
can stay. Things seem to drain in unison
      down to the field and chuckle through the gates,
things tilted from the world. The feeling's gone;
I'm left with it. I scribble with blue hands
      and head home through a car park, by fog lights.

THE FAIR THAT ALWAYS COMES

The fair that always comes
has flowered on the green. Its rides and tracks
look hammered in, and the thick gathered cables
lead away or jump unsafely up
into wild caravans.

The fair that always comes
comes early May. The land of every fair
is got to over fields on no highway.
The ground there's treacherous, the air's a gas
that seems a gas. And nothing

feels laudable or fair
until you win it and I won for you;
we slid down in a sack! Nothing is filed
or underwritten here. The safety plaque
is rusted on the wheeltop.

The fair arrives in town
at no known moment, and its hulks and girls
look through us. When they up and take the hands
of children, children trust them, the gnarled men
who make the sky go round.

I watched you go round twice,
could not help smiling, saw the names in lights
in circus letters on high scaffolding.
We ate the salt, we ate the sugar. Nighttime
rolled up popular,

and, hand in hand, five rides
we paid for. They were heights for me, to see you,
heights nobody shares or shields us from,
isolations, unawarenesses
one swivels from to find

their opposites, real shockers
nobody can deny, waiting for what
they think will scare us, faces which are all
anticipation—for the fair that comes
has come for them again,

lowered them to a blaze
they scuttle into. All we have is never
quite so narrowed down, to the nub of music
ground by force, the drone of a milieu
so faintly authorised . . .

Then the fair that always comes
is gone. No trace of you or me goes with it.
It travels miles nobody's there to measure.
Starts up again as if it never heard
what happened to us.

THE FLOOD TOWNS

At the midnight of the August day appointed,
a thousand or so
        remaining inhabitants of the doomed towns
popped champagne

at the abrupt cessation of town business,
of community
        in any legal sense, the last agreement
being that spree

till two o'clock, when all at once car headlights
lit the hillside.
        And in the morning those who had been ready
were gone,

leaving behind eight ragged families
with nowhere else
        to be, and these it would have been who heard
the very first

tinkering of rain upon the rooftops,
or saw its fingers
        spot the windows, sniffed it through the door
opened to save

the washing, and perhaps it did sound different,
the rain this time,
        not because more fierce or more aware
than former rain,

but because it fell for hours in the hearing
of folk who knew
        none in heaven or earth with any stake
in stopping it.

CHILE

Their dreams will batter open
and clack them through a turnstile
into a high stadium—
Three-legged, Sack, Pancake.
      Their mothers will be told of
      a scene of crucifixion
      the Son sat in the crowd at.

Now monologues are nightly
conducted over photos
of men in slacks and sideburns,
but he shall grow old slowly,
      treasuring the still time,
      his youngest on the mossy steps,
      a confluence of evenings;

or night when the skilled driver
will talk him home through traffic
to confinement in the country,
where dawn breaks most beautifully
      and, daily, like pink medicine,
      come gentlemen of England
      indignant at his treatment.

LOVE LETTERS FOR CELL 10

Love letters to a man
are tossed into Cell 10.
They talk about forgiveness,
requiring it of him. Ladies
dream of him the morning
he is destroyed with poison;
they burrow in the pillow.

Calamities of spotlight
crowd a lucky starlet,
lay her bare, expose her,
grown bigger in the water.
A man who dreams of change
runs smack into revenge,
is hunted to his lovelife.

The green Antarctic sun
is everything the skin
was threatened with and more.
A skeleton in care
is what it can expect,
whose one unconscious act
is where his shadow goes,

in ripples over dust.
No rest and only rest,
no ending to the sight,
no word that isn't out:
the gentleman in 10
will answer everything
the hour they get to him.

BURNING SONG

They could burn him just the once,
for in their world they burned
    anyone for burning.

They could burn him just the once,
though he burned so many people
    they needed people

to come and watch him burn.
And the more who said they would,
    the closer they came

to fairness in their world,
for if he burned alone,
    who suffered burning?

COLORADO MORNING

Looping around the more or less dead straight
lines where skiers were,

some shy, nocturnal creature's one and only
shot at its signature.

THE STRICTURES OF WHAT WAS

Nothing that's been does anything but dance.
Nothing that blinked does anything but stare,
now being over, though the merest sense
      of *over* is strange there.

They move about. The strictures of what was
are written, not enforced, so it's a faith
we could grow used to. Eyes meet other eyes,
      breath holds for breath, or breathes

to depths there never were, in bigger rooms,
for longer drives by bluer seas. What happens
has been expected and improved in dreams,
      it makes its home in seconds;

Plot is what's recalled, though there was none,
and Theme, though that's one colour of the seven
lording it awhile. Nothing's to come
      in that place—the word *heaven*

we used for something else, but the word *gone*
has what it meant in spades: an open space
the many made in us and only one
      from there could ever close.

THE SURNAMES

For Matthew Bell

There being no word to hand without its hole for light,
its origins, its loss as I set eyes on it;

there being nothing that had come to nothing else,
I took the recollected way to school and back.

It was a clear day, in that it felt cleared for this,
and hedges neat and hedges ragged passed me by.

The streets were lanes again, the houses cottages,
my life so far a daydream of a life ahead,

my life ahead at home in what had gone before,
my hands in pockets for a mile of afternoon.

These afternoons are gifted but are left alone
to dabble in the sun. The thing they leave to dry

is their own town in childhood and its look in age.
Each cottage brought a name and surname into mind.

Each surname brought a face and a recalled event
that made it catch my eye, hang like a coat of arms

a moment. At the pace I walked, the pace at which
they slip the mind, the surnames might instead have been

white crosses in a formal line, where proper nouns
and silence meet and all that comes of it are flowers.

PLAYGROUND SONG

When over the playground once they came
  to tag me It, then dance away,
I danced away and to my shame
  they're waiting for me to this day.

When I was called to answer why
  I wasn't there, I wasn't there.
All afternoon you hear them cry
  explain this at an empty chair.

When Juliet confided whom
  she loved and would I let him know,
lightheartedly I left the room,
  forgot it till an hour ago.

And tiny things too late to do
  have gone so far they can't be seen
except at dusk by me and you,
  and though I hide till Halloween

you never come, not even now
  each hand has reached the other sleeve,
not even now the light is low
  and green as you would not believe.

THE STOP AT AMHERST

For Caryl Phillips

I know my station. It's an empty room
with doors at either end, with a typed sheet
that tells you times, a bench
to wait on when it rains,
and a clock to keep an eye on,
if only tit-for-tat. It shares the building

with a shop for stamp collectors, who are there
at other times entirely. I'd be there
if everything were changed
and I mean everything,
so, if you see me there,
absorbed, I would suggest you get out quickly.

I check the times for north, my finger glides
up Greenland to the Pole, then backtracks down
to the familiar names.
When it meets the very town
I'm standing in, a pulse
locates me: something meets itself in horror,

and on I go most steadily to southward,
Connecticut, New York—I hear a screech
of life at that, move down
into unvisited
polysyllabic towns,
San this, San that; I follow arrows somewhere

unpronounceable, torn off, no help.
I step out to the platform, where a group
has stood for ages, posed
in quiet rearrangements
each time I look, as if
I can't stop finding angles, but I swear

I never move, it's them. Old men alone,
families rotating, lovers kissing,
having you believe
they're both oblivious
to everyone, when look:
they won't forget this when it's all they had.

There are no fences by the line, no fences
at the crossing. I could run a stoplight
and face the Polar night train
in baking sunshine. Well,
another time. That whistle
shivered a quatrain of Emily's,

and here comes the great double-deckered silver
missile-shaped design. High-panelled walls
from all the other worlds
slide deafeningly by.
A man in uniform
detaches from a door and in the darkness

everybody's relatives. The rails
to north and south have vanished for the time
the finger passes over
the name that's everybody's,
but I will sweat it out,
will seem suspicious, be the one they saw

not joining it, not leaving it, not finding
anyone to meet, not giving up
a single soul to it.
I'll meet the children's eyes,
the train conductor's eyes,
stay rooted to the town whose name I'm growing

all about me on my dusty strip.
The world inches away from me. I breathe it
out of sight. I leave
the station: by a shortcut
I'll reach the town. No need
to cross that dusty and deserted room

with the typed sheet, the wooden bench to wait on,
the clock: to do so is to be somehow
exactly where what comes
will look, and, set against
that place, even the past
is on my doorstep, beaming with surprises.

THE SNOW VILLAGE

In the age of pen and paper,
when the page was a snow village,
when days the light was leafing through
descended without message,

the nib that struck from heaven
was the sight of a cottage window
lit by the only certain
sign of a life, a candle,

glimpsed by a stranger walking
at a loss through the snow village.
All that can flow can follow
that sighting, though no image,

no face appear—not even
the hand that draws across it—
though the curtains close the vision,
though the stranger end his visit,

though the snow erase all traces
of his passage through the village,
though his step become unknowable
and the whiteness knowledge.